Goings Rules of Racism

My Rules & Theories of Racism from The Unaware Realities That I See

I0767419

"It ought to be possible, in short, for every American to enjoy the privileges of being American without regard to his race or his color. In short, every American ought to have the right to be treated as he would wish to be treated, as one would wish his children to be treated."

- John F. Kennedy

Preston A Goings

ISBN 9798882984464:

This book is dedicated to those who have been seared by the intense heat of racism. I am sorry. The reason I wrote this book is to help with eradicating racism for all time!

– Preston A Goings

CONTENTS

Preface

Warning! First, I would like to say, please use caution while reading this book. I tell you this because it may make you view things differently than how you previously did.

The reason I wrote this book is because I am faced with racism everywhere I go. If it's not direct racism, it's indirect racism. You will know the difference when you encounter them. On Confronting indirect racism website[1], it describes direct and indirect racism as "Direct racism occurs when something obvious and blatant is said or done, while indirect racism occurs when something subtle or covert occurs." I wrote this book so that you can understand what racism is and what my theory of racism is, the cause, the end of racism, and what to do when faced with racism...so, what do you do if you are faced with racism? This book will answer this question for you.

Racism is a hard topic to discuss at times. Some people have that fire within them to speak up about it and some people hold it in. Unfortunately, that's when health problems can happen. A 2019 research review found negative associations between reports of racial discrimination and many physical and mental health conditions, as well as preclinical indicators for disease. These include cardiovascular disease, coronary artery calcification, mental health disorder (e.g., depression, anxiety disorders, post-traumatic stress disorder, eating disorders, and psychosis) obesity, hypertension (high blood pressure) alcohol use and misuse, engaging in high-risk behaviors, poorer sleep, inflammation, and cortisol dysregulation (a hormone that regulates stress levels in the body) [1]

This book is not only for my own racial group. I am a black man. Even though my people and I deal with a lot of racism for several unbelievable reasons. I wrote this book for all the Blacks, Indigenous, and people of color out there, and people that are dealing with racial discrimination in the United States of America and around the world.

Please, before you dive into this book. I want you to take your time and do a Goings Rules of Racism experiment 1, found on the next page. At the end of this book there will be another Goings Rules of Racism experiment 2. Please use a pencil to go through these, as you may want to share this book with someone else. On these experiments, don't take too much time trying to figure it out what to write. Just react to whatever comes to your mind first. After the second experiment you will get the results and the reasons from how you answered.

There is no right or wrong answer when you're doing the experiments. There will be an explanation of each choice answered. Please don't take what you answer to heart. I only want you to realize the theory that I am trying to convey to you. Please take in all I have written. At times you may have to pause for a moment to reflect, and that's normal because I did the same. Everything that I want to make known to you is from my heart so take it and embrace it.

GOINGS RULES OF RACISM
EXPERIMENT 1

Circle # 1 **Circle # 2** **Circle # 3**

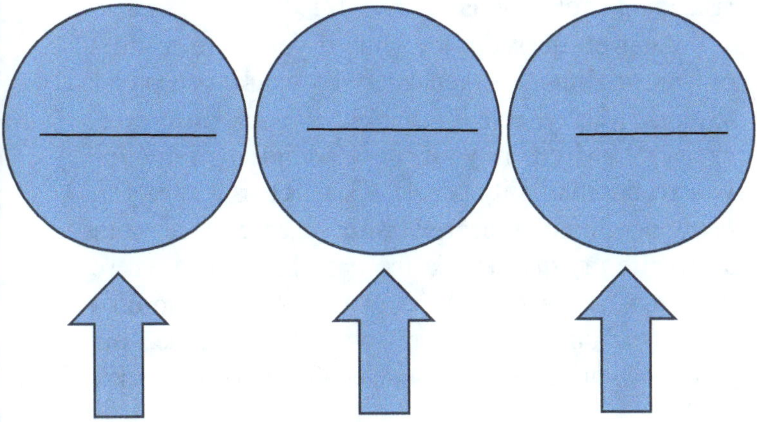

What is your own race?	Your best friend's race or a race you're familiar with?	What is a race you never collaborated with?

Answer here ________________

The questions are: 1) What is your own race? 2) What is your best friend's race or a race you're familiar with? 3) What is a race you have never collaborated with? In the last question, I am essentially saying a race you have never gotten to know or talk with before. Please fill in your answers inside the circles please.

Another question for you: If you were to do a project or a business venture, who would you prefer to do it with? Circle #1, which is **your own race**, circle #2, which is **your best friend or someone you're familiar with**, circle #3, which is **a race you have never collaborated with**. Please write your answer to the question in the underlined area where the arrow is pointing. Who would you want to do a project or business venture with, for example, put Circle #1, or circle #2, or circle #3. Please only pick one!

Theory of What Causes Future Racism

VISUAL PERCEPTIONS

So, what are visual perceptions? Long story short, it is the ability to see and interpret one's visual environment.[2]

Now let's look at the family environment, your self-image, and past events.

I am going to explain to you in detail my theory of what causes future racism. I am going to have a section for three of the Goings Rules of Racism formulas, which are past experiences, present thinking, no thinking, or observation. This formula will be applied to the family environment, one's self-image, and past events, so that you can get an understanding of the solution, which is to have no future racism.

After I am finished with my theory on what causes future racism, I will give my formula or theory as to what will end future racism - the solution.

What causes **future racism**? Below is my formula that causes future racism, while connecting it with your family environment.

(Future racism = past experiences + present thinking + non-thinking or no self-observation)

Family Environment

Past experiences

Do you remember any moments in the past that you had with your family? Please take a moment to reflect on those moments. Focus on positive moments.

Okay back to the book! Now I bet some of your memories that you thought of made you feel happy, sad, or maybe even angry. But to keep things on a positive note, I really hope you picked out a happy memory with your family. I believe that this is one of the factors involved in people being racist and showing racism. For example, you showed platonic intimacy, personal interaction, and trust at one time with your family, or even still do so now. Well, these are the three formulas from Goings Rules of Racism.

(**Trust** = personal interaction + platonic Intimacy)

Everything that you saw with your family - their personalities, their skin tone, their hair type, their eye shape etc. - these few things, as I mentioned, look exactly like yours or very similar to yours.

When you were with your family, and only your close family members, during a barbecue gathering, eating dinner together, or a family reunion, you had the same personal interaction with them all the time and that is what you are used to. You are comfortable with that. You will probably feel uncomfortable with a non-family member person that looks different than your family to spend some personal interaction with, especially if they speak a whole different language. If you can't speak their language and they can't speak your language this creates a barrier with others that can lead to racism.

Having platonic intimacy with one of your family members most likely means one of the greatest things to you. You may be having a bad day, you could have lost a family member inside your family tree, or you may have broken up with a boyfriend or girlfriend and you need someone to talk to. And there you remember that one family member that sat down and listened to your every word. This could have been a cousin, mother, or father that had open ears for your feelings to be heard.

These two subjects that I explained, personal interaction and platonic intimacy all build up to the ultimate solution, Trust. Trust is the main reason you talked to one of, or maybe multiple members of, your family. As you trusted your family you were talking with, you looked at each other. You may not know this, but you see their skin, their eyes, and maybe the way they talk; their accent.

Untimely, this is something that happened in your past that you sincerely remember. You didn't have personal interaction, platonic intimacy, and trust with a different nonmember of your family. For instance, you may not have had a personal interaction with someone that is not a family member and possibly from another race - for example, someone from Africa, the United States, Mexico, just to name a few.

Unfortunately, since you haven't had that personal interaction, platonic intimacy, or trust with that person that is different from your family, I believe that this is what causes the seed of racism to occur. You're so used to the way things happen with your family, as well as the visual perception that you're used to. It could have been happening the same way for years. Over and over, you know who exactly to go to when you need a shoulder to cry on with one of your family members, therefore, you get comfortable.

Present thinking

Your visual perception of what you see now affects your social life because of what you are used to being around. When you are outside your comfort zone your mind is stuck in the past of what you remembered visually seeing. This can cause racism to flourish. This is because this is all you know. Your brain only acts on what it deciphers, recognizes, and memorizes.[3]

It is like something that you do repeatedly. A lot of people are not aware of it and some people are aware of it. At times some people do things without thinking about it because it has been embedded inside of their minds. I've noticed that when you do something repeatedly you start becoming like it. For example, if you were to take a flight out to Jamaica and live there for six or nine months, and you then come back to where you used to live, you might have an accent of the Jamaicans. You will maybe pick up some of their ways and traditions.

When it comes to present thinking, and out into a social environment, you will interpret people from your past thinking. What I mean by that is your family member(s) that you have seen when you spent time in personal interaction with, had a deep platonic intimacy with, and trust. This is the primary way you will feel comfortable around people that you presently see. When you feel comfortable around people that you may meet - for example, a classmate or coworker at a large firm - you will experience personal interaction and growing platonic intimacy, which leads to trust towards them.

Lastly, past experiences with your family and present thinking of your family may make you not want to be around a different kind of person, have a conversation, or invite them to hang out with your group of family members. You will not give that person, that is different from your visual perception of your family, your personal interaction, your platonic intimacy, and your trust because that person doesn't look and/or act like someone from your family that you felt comfortable being around.

When someone looks different than who your family looks like then you might not ask that individual if they want to hang out at the bar with your other friends. I believe this is all because of your visual perception of what you see of another person.

Non-thinking or no self-observation

For many of us, when you are around your family you act differently than when you are around people on the outside. When you are around your family you get so used to doing their customs, believing in their beliefs, and your visual perception of them. This is all because this was what you were around ever since you were a baby. And this is how you think. Most people don't think about other people and their beliefs.

You are like being on auto pilot all the time and not paying attention to yourself and your actions. For example, how you may shake one of your family members' hands compared to a stranger's hand. If you shake someone's hand, not opening to people of different ethnic groups, with no love, sincere, or respect, this could be the start of being racist.

It all boils down to this, if you are using this section of Goings Rules of Racism, non-thinking or no self-observation when you meet a different person in a racial or ethnic group than you may become racist toward them. Because the worst thing that can ever happen to you is to not be aware that you are racist. Even when you don't want to be racist. This may take a moment to sink in.

The Three Organs

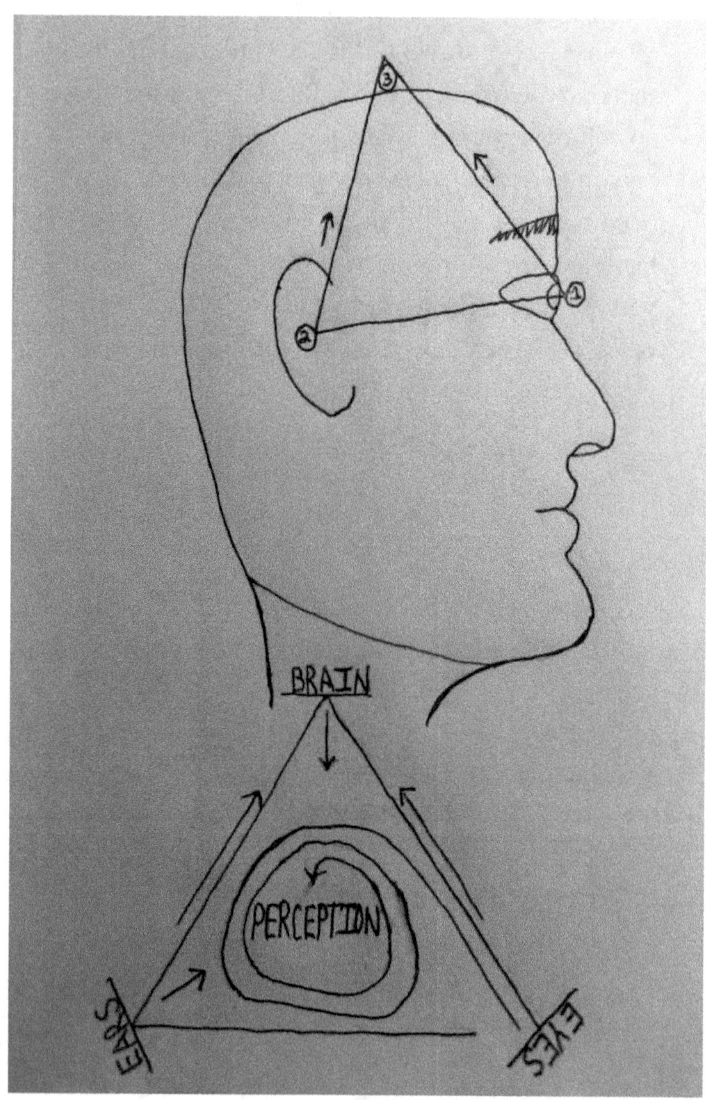

This picture illustrates the concept of the three organs. Notice the numbers one through three are at the top of the drawing of the person's head. 3 represents the human brain, 2 represents the human ears, and 1 represents the human eyes.

At the bottom of the picture, you will notice I have the three human organs - eyes, ears, and brain. In the center there is the word perception. I have it this way because with these three human organs this will create a person's perception of situations, making the individual take actions based on their perceptions. What I mean by action is the action each person takes from the three organs they have analyzed. All the data that was received from the three organs eyes, ears, and brain. Once the brain concludes, we will make thoughts and actions that follow after, ultimately determining if he or she is a racist individual or not.

With the ears, eyes, and brain all working together to make a perception of each individual's own reality. Starting with the eyes first, then following the ears, the brain takes these inputs and analyzes them. Once the brain analyzes what it sees and hears it will then make decisions based on what is heard and what is constantly being seen through the eyes.

Your Self-Image

Remember what causes **future racism**? Again, below is my formula that I believe causes future racism, connecting it with your self-image.

(Future racism = past experiences + present thinking + non-thinking or no self-observation)

Your self-image, according to Berkeley Well-Being Institute, can be define as a person's perception of themselves, including their physical appearance, personality, and characteristics.[4]

Past experiences

You do not realize this but when you look at yourself in the mirror multiple times you start to believe this is who you are. But in actuality it's not. It's just your surface appearance. There are so many things about yourself that you don't know and maybe you do know and you need to change. Mostly, it all revolves around who you hang around with. Look at their skin tone, their personality, and their beliefs. When it comes to your friends' and family's beliefs you could simply ask them what they believe about other races of people. If they are racist, for example, you could ask one of your friends what do you think about black people. What would you do if they respond, "I hate them Niggers." If they respond this way ask them why? When you figure out why they hate black people, and you are saying to yourself that you do not hate any race, especially black people, then this person may not be the best person to be your friend. You may have to cut off all ties with this person, because if not you will become a little bit like them without knowing it. You could intentionally become as they are or subconsciously become as they are, or you could work with them on their prejudices.

I believe this is true, for instance, as I mentioned before, if you go to Jamaica and live there for six months and come back to the United States. You may have a Jamaican accent and perhaps not be aware of it. We are beings that adapt to whatever we are around for long periods of time. It's just something that happens naturally. This saying comes in perfectly with this subject and I know you heard this saying before, or something similar to it: "Beware of who you hang around with, because if they get in trouble you can get in trouble with them." A bad influence!

Now after all this is said and done, because of your lack of awareness you will act more like your friend and others you hang out with for long periods of time. If you're only going by the memories of fun times, and it is the reason you repeatedly see and hang around your friends and not analyze the situation, then your self-image will gradually become more of the same. If you think about it, you don't know if you're racist or not if you're never aware of your actions upon people you meet. I do believe that there is a such thing as people being racist and not even knowing it, or aware of their own behavior.

What if you had a broken family, such as a broken mother or father. What I mean by broken is that your mother or father neglected you, treated you very bad, or they were a failure in life and never pursued any career or something that you could look up to when you were lost and confused on what you wanted to do in life.

I trust that this will affect you because it will make you dislike yourself because you see the image of your failed parents in yourself.

So now let's say you're out in society and you run into someone that is of your own race. You may not react to them as you would to another race. This is because it reminds you of an experience in the past that you want to get away from. I believe this is how people show racism against their own race.

Present thinking

What I mean by present thinking is the way you are thinking now compared to three years, six years, or maybe even nine years ago. The way you think now is very important to your self-image. If you're not aware of your actions, then there will never be a change in you or anyone else in this world. Most every move you make and every decision you take is basically all from your past thoughts and experiences. All this and more are all how you interpret everything around you. Whatever race you are.

Now imagine that you go up to someone not of your own race, but a different race of people. Would you do it? If you said no, then most likely it is because you haven't done something like that in your past, so you're not doing it now in your present time. You will most likely ignore them or walk around them.

It is like going in a circle repeatedly and never knowing any other direction to take because you just don't know. This is what I call people that don't think outside the box. These are people that are presently thinking about bad and sour past experiences.

Non-thinking or no self-observation

When it comes to non-thinking or no self-observation, I trust this is very important when it involves your self-image. Let use the Japanese people for an example. They don't usually shake hands during business meetings or in general they nod their head in what is called bowing. If you didn't know it or understand it, you could get offended if they didn't shake your hand the way others that you may have known for years do. And the Japanese may get offended because you didn't bow towards them after they have bowed first to you.

Not being aware of your actions could be the number one cause of racism spreading throughout the United States of America Maybe throughout the whole world. The most dangerous thing you can do is to do something to offend someone and not know that you did it. A lot of us do not think when we ask questions of another race or when we interact with them. We never take time to think to ask if this question is going to offend this person if I say this or that? Most of us don't think when we speak. For example, The little Mermaid movie. We all know that the little Mermaid movie in the past was this animated movie. Millions of people were used to seeing this character, which is a white woman, skinny, and with long straight red hair. This falls under Goings Rules of Racism formula; future racism=past experiences + present thinking + non-thinking or no self-observation. Most likely when the movie first came out everyone wanted to look like that image of Ariel - the Mermaid. Thirty-four years later they made a real movie of The Little Mermaid with actual people and not cartoons. Ariel is replaced by a black girl with the casting of actress

Halle Bailey as the main character Ariel, and a lot of people disagreed with that, often because they are racist. They did not like the fact that her skin was dark, and she looked different from the original Ariel. If they were to use a foreign person that looks white there would have not been any controversy at all.

Over in China and South Korea, that Ariel was portrayed by a black woman, this somehow caused a lot of controversy. On CNN an article I came across, "'The little Mermaid' tanks in China and South Korea amid racist backlash from some viewers." A piece in the article says,

"Disney's live-action remake has made only $3.6 million in mainland China since opening there on May 26, according to Box Office Mojo.

It brought in just 19.5 million yuan ($2.7 million) in its first five days, compared with 142 million yuan (nearly $20 million) for "Spider-Man: Across the Spider-Verse" in the first five days of that film's opening, according to Chinese box office tracker Endata.

In South Korea, "The Little Mermaid" has grossed $4.4 million since May 24.

The movie attracted some 472,000 viewers in its first week in theaters there, less than the 643,000 fans who showed up for new "Fast and Furious" film "Fast X," over the same duration, according to the Korean Film Council. "Fast X" opened a week before "The Little Mermaid""".[5]

That was a terrible thing not only for the movie when they did a movie targeting of alleged 'review bombing' but for the actress herself. I think that no one that was involved in this ever thought how the actress Halle Bailey felt. Not only that but to the millions of black girls out there, how did they feel? And to the millions of black boys out there, how did they feel about the discouragement of race controversy. This should make you ask the question, 'if by chance thirty-four years ago they would have shown a black Ariel, would all this race controversy happen?'

After hearing a white man say what I am about to tell you, it made me wonder what was said in the United States about this situation. There was a white man that said to a black person, if it was a white woman then this movie would have made more money." Now that saying could have really offended the black man. And the black man could have thought the white man was racist for saying that. But it could have been something that he was used to seeing. He was in his late forties in age, and he was talking like that. This is all due to his visual perceptions of the way he sees things in his past, therefore, he still sees them the same way. There are ways that we are all the same. If you look at the picture on the next page, you will find that we are more similar than you can imagine.

We all have these things: human Organs, human digestive system, skeletal system, cells and nervous system. All these special parts of the human body makes us the same.

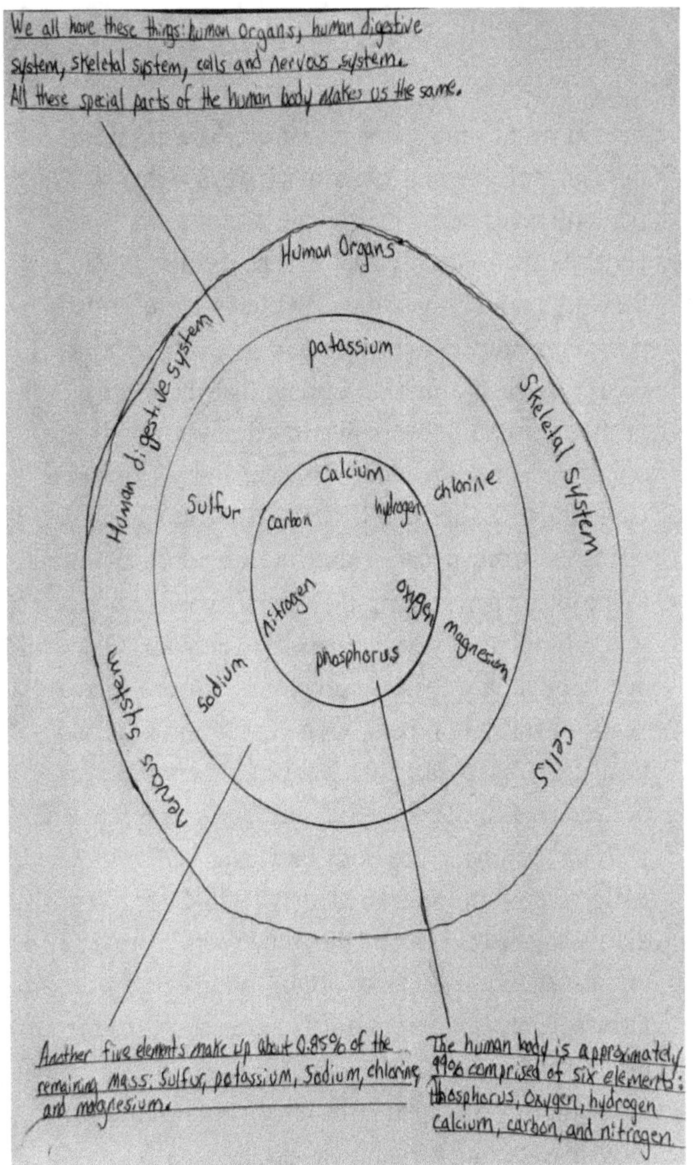

Another five elements make up about 0.85% of the remaining mass: Sulfur, potassium, Sodium, chlorine, and magnesium.

The human body is approximately 99% comprised of six elements: Phosphorus, Oxygen, hydrogen, calcium, carbon, and nitrogen.

Past Events

In past events people that are fifty-eight through seventy-six years old have a higher visual perception of being racist than the other generations. I believe that this holds true because of the way people's visual perceptions were in their past compared to the other two generations' past - Gen X and Millennials. I know that there are probably more generations, but I am going to use only three of them, which are the Baby Boomers, Generation X, and the Millennials. I am going to use these three because they are the most important to the other generation, the Gen Z, younger, generation, ages seven through twenty-six. I got this age through a website jasondorsey.com.[6] It gave the years of Baby boomers, Gen X, Millennials, and Gen Z. The site said that Baby boomers are born between 1946-1964, Gen X are born between 1965-1976, Millennials are born between 1977-1995 and lastly, Gen Z are born between 1996-2015. When I did the math on each of the birth years from 2022 my results are as follows. Baby boomer ages are from seventy-six through fifty-eight (at the time of this writing), Gen X ages are from fifty-seven through forty-six, and Millennials ages are from forty-five through twenty-seven.

We all know that when each generation has children, they only teach them what they know.

Therefore, if that generation, specifically baby boomers were racist then their children may believe their parent's values and then they may spread the racism down to the generations to come.

In this section I am going to use Goings Rules of Racism formula to explain the reason people are racist through their visual perceptions that they see. (Future racism = past experiences + present thinking + non-thinking or no self-observation)

Past experiences

Older people, for instance Baby Boomers, ages seventy-six through fifty-eight may have become set in their old ways of only wanting and interacting with people of their own kind. What I mean by this is people that have the same skin tone, eyes, hair, culture, and economic status. This can cause a massive racist pandemic for the Baby Boomers. This disease can be so strong that it could stick in the minds of Gen X, Millennials, and Gen Z. Alternatively, if parents build a healthy relationship and communication with their children, it's possible their children could reach back to them with new, lest racist, belief patterns.

I believe this holds true because we as human parents typically discipline our children the same way our parents discipline us. If in the past our parents used to yell at us, curse at us, and say that they hate a certain race out there, then it's possible the next generation will copy their parents' ways because they don't know any better. But if Gen X and Millennials saw their parents be really kind and showed them how to make money, how to interact with people, how to not be closed off when it comes to other cultures and different races, then Gen Z will start a great trend of not being racist and one day eliminate racism all together.

Another example is business. Some of you that are reading this, maybe your parents started a restaurant of your race name. What I mean by this is Mexican, Italian, Chinese, Korean, etc., just to name a few. And as you were around your parents, you noticed that they were a sophisticated businessman or sophisticated businesswoman. Maybe they hire only their kind and no other race but takes the money of all races and feeds them. You see this for years. Maybe you've even seen a person fill out an application and seen one of the coworkers toss it in the trash because of who he or she's race was. The point that I am getting at is after your parents become older and want to keep the restaurant in the family you will most likely take over the business. Ask yourself this question - would you run the restaurant the same way as your parent(s) did? Your answer will likely be yes because you know that they know more about the business in the past than you did.

Unfortunately, if this type of behavior persists

in the United States and around the world, racism will possess every racial group around the world. Just image that for the future of this planet. How are we going to make this world a better place while being divided by racism?

Present thinking

As I mentioned in the recent past experiences section your present thinking is caused by your past experiences. This has been going on for years and years - from generations that have passed away to the new generation of people that are taking their spot. For example, I came across a woman and she told me that she hates all Mexicans. I asked her why you hate all Mexicans. She answered back, "Because a Mexican killed my sister and fled the country to go back to Mexico." When using this example just imagine this woman telling her story to her family, people she interacts with, her friends, her children. So now her family, people that she interacted with and told the story to, friends, and children all are going to have that in the back of their minds, figuratively speaking.

Let's just use her children for an example. The woman tells her children, and her children digest this story. The sad thing about it all is if they run into Mexicans now, they are going to be thinking about this. This will probably make them racist toward them, and this racism toward them will trickle down through generations and generations to come. Then later when this woman's children have children, the children will continue on with a reason why they dislike Mexicans.

Another good example of how the past can make you racist through visual perceptions and through past events is what you've seen on the mainstream media. Not only that but TikTok and Instagram videos as well - social media. When people watch videos, they see different kinds of people of different races doing things that are sexual and what is considered sinful. For instance, twerking, wearing very tight clothing, wearing very little clothing, and doing body sex gestures. People from different countries start to believe that the whole ethnic group of people are like that. There was this article I came across titled, *"I'd always fantasized about living in Japan. But after nearly 3 years of living here as a Black woman, I'm ready to move back to the US."*[7] Her name is Renee Marant. She was a college student that was living in Japan. She had low job prospects and some experiences with racism. I am going to point out the racism topic because I am using this as an example for this book. In a small section of this article what really stood out to me was the experiences with racism section. Renee mentioned, *"One of the downsides of living in Japan as a black woman is the fetishization that we face. I've observed that Japanese people often view black women as being "sexually free," and I've encountered a lot of men who have harassed me because they think I'm that way. I think a lot of these ideas come from the way black women are portrayed in the media.*

For example, I've had men come up to me and touch me, ask me if I like Megan Thee Stallion, and ask if I can twerk. It's really frustrating and dehumanizing to be treated this way, and it makes me feel like I'm not being seen as a person but just as a sexual object."

That man that came up to Renee Marant sexually harassed her and asked if she could twerk and if she liked Megan Thee Stallion only knows what he saw about her through the mainstream media. His mind was stuck in the past, therefore, this poisonous way of thinking still exists within his present thinking mind.

Let's say he is in the Generation X category. It is a strong possibility that his children will think the way he does. And if that's the case their children will take on that same mindset that their parents placed into their minds. And it will continue on, over and over, through generation after generation to come. They will all be encapsulated by the horrors of racism.

Non-thinking or no self-observation

Sometimes you can come across multiple different people that are of different ethnic groups than what you are. The reason why I am mentioning this is because a bad past event can trigger the way someone thinks this is true if they use non-thinking and or no self-observation in their social life. For instance, road rage. You are out driving on the road, and you get cut off by a person of a different racial group. The person yells at you, cusses you out, and almost runs you off the road. What if that triggers something in the back of your mind when you see another person of that same ethnic group? perhaps you act rude to them, as if they were the one that created that crazy chaos on the road. This situation could spread like the Black Death plague.

I believe in every ethnic group there is that one person that acts like they are racist in some way, shape, or form. Maybe they came across a situation like I mentioned, or they saw something on social media, and it disgusted them, and they believe that all people of that racial group behave in a rude, unmoral, and overwhelmingly sexual way.

Not all people are the same. Some people are different. We must understand that just because someone that is of a different racial group does not represent your bad past encounters with that racial group.

Theory of What Causes no Future Racism

What causes **no future racism**? Below is my formula that I believe causes no future racism.

(No Future Racism = past experiences + change in present thinking + thinking or self-observing)

In this part of section one, I am going to talk about how my theory, using my formula, eliminates future racism.

I am going to go through each section of the visual perceptions. The subtitle subjects I will cover are family environment, your self-image, and past events. This is going to be the same topics being covered earlier, but in this section, I will give my theories on no future racism. I will apply my formula (no future racism = past experiences + change in present thinking + thinking or self-observing). I believe and trust that if this theory is applied the right way to the three situations of family environment, your self-image, and past events, there will be no future racism.

Family Environment

Past experiences

Can you imagine a future without racism in it, or a future where racism towards people is so limited that we all, as a people of this world, forget that it ever existed. I truly believe it is possible. I like most of what I said first - a future without racism in it! Doesn't it sound so good saying it out loud, or even just thinking about it?

Family is a great thing to have close if they are loving and respectful. If everyone in the world sees everyone as family just imagine how different this world could be in the future. Honestly, I believe it is not a hard thing to do. We are not that different from one another, besides skin tone, hair texture, parts of our body that are different in shapes and sizes.

Now when we think with a higher level of intelligence, we will start to see the very thing that makes us all the same. We have bowel movements, we have a heart that pumps blood, we have cells in our bodies that heals our skin when it gets fractured, we eat food when we are hungry, our digestive system digests the food and our body absorbs all that it needs from it.

If we could all speak one language, then the future will be less racist than what it is now. I trust that different languages block us from communicating properly, kindly, and lovingly with one another. Communication is key to the beginning of any relationship. Either it's a step to finding true love, as well as a step to breaking the ice to understand someone or an entire racial group. The way this technology is going at this time that there is no excuse to not want to learn another language or learn about another culture. There are so many language apps out there it is mind-boggling to comprehend. Once you start searching for language apps you'll be overwhelmed by how many there are.

I truly believe that once we are willing to educate ourselves on different cultures, languages, and socioeconomic statuses, we ourselves, people that are knowingly racist and don't care, people that are racist and not know, it will not be racist any more. This also goes for the people that encountered someone from a different ethnic group that that had an experience that was terrible, so now they hate the entire ethnic group.

Change present thinking

You have to change the present thinking that you currently have. For example, the very first step you need to take is to consciously seek to change your present thinking. This needs to happen because you need to get out of your comfort zone. I am sure you've probably heard this before, and it is true. We tend to get in our comfort zones when we are around family using my trust formula (trust = personal interaction + platonic intimacy.) You get very comfortable with this formula when you only apply it to your past family. Keep in mind doing this over and over again will shape you and mold you into what you are. In some cases, this could be happening to you and you don't even realize it. I am not saying that this is a bad thing, but I believe that it only becomes bad when you are not aware and not willing to change your present thinking.

Imagine that one day you decide to change your present thinking and start observing what you do every day. It will be sad if one day you do this and come to the conclusion that you are racist. Think about it. What would you do? Take a moment to think about this one. If you're not sure what to think about then read this entire book and you will know for sure if you were racist or not. I believe that there are people who are unaware if they are racist, as well as some people that are racist and know they are racist and still continue to be that way. But for the people out there that don't know that they are racist it is time to change your present way of thinking. Now! Now! Now! I trust the only way this world will get rid of racism is if people change their present way of thinking. It will start by changing the present way of thinking for one person at a time.

You will know if you are thinking in a racist way because it will be negative thinking towards people different from your own racial group. For instance, thinking that everyone in a different racial group than you are criminals just because you see them on television doing criminal acts. You have to believe that not everyone in that racial group is the negative that you saw. It could be totally the opposite.

Thinking or self-observing

We as a people need to think and self-observe ourselves. We as a people need to consider that this world that we live in isn't only what we see in the mirror. It is a world filled with different kinds of people of many different shapes, sizes, colors, hair types, personality types, cultures, and socioeconomic backgrounds.

Take the time to study different racial groups. Figure out their situations before judging them. I trust if you do this, every encounter with them will be different than not knowing anything about them. I believe you will see things differently. I believe you will show a different type of respect towards them. This goes back to the trust formula. Trust = personal interaction + platonic intimacy.

Before you can make it to the trust formula you will have to get to know the other racial group of people and understand them first. Then after you have done so trust will become something for everyone as a group of people. You may one day follow this instruction and find yourself becoming friends with someone of a different ethnic group than what you are. Once this happens then you will most likely use the trust formula as your relationship with that individual grows. Then in a great miraculous way you will see all the people of that person's racial group in a different perspective. Just imagine - large groups of people from different countries wouldn't have anything to say about the movie, 'The Little Mermaid,' as we talked about earlier in this book. But there'd be great news of how much of a great actress Halle Bailey is and the wonderful performance that she performed. There could be a Chinese or Asian Ariel, a Mexican Ariel, a Korean Ariel, an Indian Ariel and so on in the near future. No one would have something to say about what racial group is playing Ariel's character from 'The Little Mermaid' movie. This, I trust, could be possible if Goings Rules of Racism's theory of no future racism = past experiences + change in present thinking + thinking & self-observing were applied to everyday life in the United States and around the whole world. Then there would be no future racism. In the future, racism would no longer exist.

Your Self-Image

Past experiences

When you go deeper into this book your awareness will for sure open wider. Once that happens a friend or family member(s) may not have the open awareness of racism you will have. Therefore, beware of the clash that may accrue. For example, say you have been knowing a person for a very long time and your awareness of racism expands, but you notice that your friend is racist. So, what do you do? That is something to think about. You most likely have that trust with them (Trust = personal interaction + platonic intimacy). You may have that trust with your best friend or family member, and it has been going on for years. I say that the best solution to this problem is to enlighten your friend or family member(s) to understanding what causes future racism. If they don't understand, then they may not be the right person(s) to hang around with or be around with in general.

If you can change your friend(s) or family member(s) visual perceptions on life on how they view different racial groups, then we are making progress towards a better world, which is no future racism! It must start somewhere right? Once this greatness spreads throughout the whole world, there will be no future racism in existence.

You know now what you are doing and what has

happened to you in past experiences. You must be aware now that every bad experience in your past with another racial group doesn't mean the whole racial group is that way. You should know now that everything you repeatedly did in your past affects your present. I won't go into too much detail about this subject matter because I will be talking about it in the next title subject. So, when you repeatedly do something with someone that you are hanging around with you will subconciously become like them. This will happen because if you're not aware of your subconscious mind then you will act suddenly based on what will be downloaded *into* your subconscious mind.

So, what is the subconscious mind? According to the Collins dictionary, 'Your subconscious is the part of your mind that can influence you or affect your behavior even though you are not aware of it.'[8]

On a site entitled, Reporter.rit.edu, there is an article that is titled, "Secrets of the Subconscious."[9]. Inside that article it says that according to Chad Chesmark, "Our subconscious mind is constantly working behind the scenes. It's what keeps us breathing when we sleep. It stores all our memories, habits, fears, and phobias."

This is an interesting article because as I mentioned to you earlier in this book your past experiences can create the possibility that you could be racist. Perhaps you were around a family member(s) and they always talked about another racial group's imperfections and had not figured out why by doing some research and investigating. When this happens around you this gets stored in your memories, habits, fears, and phobias, and when you get around someone of a different ethnicity group you start to react to them without realizing your behavior.

To counteract this, you need to be aware of your past experiences by thinking about what has happened in your past, and if there is something that you find that is racist from another person. Or maybe just changing your behavior is the greatest solution that could happen. By you changing your feelings away from your past experiences you can move forward without having a racist thought in your mind. Especially your subconscious mind.

If this could happen to all the people around the world, starting inside the United States of American, my own home, then there would be no future racism. The Goings Rules of Racism formula for no future racism will be the cure to the present racism.

Change present thinking

Present thinking and past experiences go hand in hand. If you can control your past experiences of thought that will change your present thinking, then you can become something great. If you don't have children now then your children can be taught this by you or if you already have children then you can change their present thinking.

When you look at yourself in the mirror, please look and say a few words while looking directly at yourself. Wave at yourself with the best smile you can produce. Really observe your ears, the size of your head, the shape of your body, your eyes, your hair. After you are finished just think - there are people out there in the world that would not understand what you just said or your expression of saying hi, or the image that they see. There are people out there that do not look the way you do. There are people out there that have a different color than you do.

Now there are a large group of people that may look like you and will understand your smile and understand your expression of saying hi to them. They may even reflect what you just did. You smile, they smile, you wave they wave, you say, 'hi, how are you?' and they say the same thing. You will most likely feel comfortable with this and express trust to them or express the beginning of the start of the trust formula, which is trust = personal interaction + platonic intimacy.

Thinking or self-observing

When you start thinking and self-observing, you get a harmonic feeling of peace inside and out of yourself. What I mean by this is when you start being aware of different racial groups than what you are, you begin to understand things and you will have peace. You won't have those thoughts of bad past experiences that are keeping you from being how you truly could be, which which could be loving. And using the formula of trust with every person that you meet. No matter what their color, culture, or socioeconomic status. You will use that trust formula (Trust = personal interaction + platonic intimacy) to socialize with people. Keep in mind that it will take time for each part that makes up trust, for instance, personal interaction coming first frequently. When it comes to platonic intimacy, that part takes time because an individual must keep doing the personal interaction repeatedly before it turns into platonic intimacy.

Like I mentioned in your self-image for the future racism formula. What causes it is not thinking about other peoples' feelings and not self-observing your actions as well as your thoughts. When you get to that level and take full advantage of it all this will get downloaded into your subconscious mind. Once these magnanimous actions get planted into your subconscious mind then you will naturally be a non-racist, great person. When you become this person, people around you will want to be like you, and then this greatness can spread around the world.

When you find free time try doing some studying of a different ethnic group and study their culture, their socioeconomic status, and their background. Do some deeper research for yourself by attending organized culture events that are different from your own, and while you are there ask them questions to get a better understanding. Ask what will offend you while having a conversation with someone? You will be surprised at what they will have to say. Ask, "Do you feel that there is racism happing to you and your ethnic group?" Just listen and don't interrupt. Just listen to them. If you feel that you need to review this later, you could ask to record the conversation or take a pen and piece of paper for taking notes.

Past Events

In this section I am going to use the Goings Rules of Racism formula to explain the ways there could be no future racism. (<u>No future racism</u> = past experiences + change in present thinking + thinking or self-observation)

Past experiences

Parents are the most important demographic when it comes to no future racism. They are the most important because they are the ones that have been around their children. And children look up to their parents. Children put all their trust in their parents. They most likely now emulate them on how they discipline, how they cook, how they clean, how they treat other ethnic groups. If children see that their parents were kind and understanding to other racial groups, then they will be kind and understanding as well. Then they can pass down that type of attitude to their children, and so on.

If parents are currently racist, what they will have to do is change their perception on what happened to them in the past. They will need to teach their children that it is not okay to be racist toward your own race or towards another race that's different than your own. They must sit their children down to explain to them the reason why they should not be racist. They must explain that this world will not be a better place if racism exists.

Things happen in the past all the time. You may be at a bus stop, gas station pumping gas, at a bar or wherever you are, and you may get someone that does something overly disrespectful to you. For instance, they may yell at you or tease you, or maybe do something to you to make you believe they are racist towards you. It is totally up to you to spread the racist and disrespectfulness to another person or cut it off. You can say to yourself, "That person could be having a bad day. He or she is not perfect. He or she doesn't know better." You must continue to think and realize what happened in their past. Something that happened to that individual's past is the reason that they may be acting out this way.

When you come across racist situations, maybe someone saying a racial slur to you, you will have to think in a different way. Ask yourself what they have been exposed to as a child. It is a bad feeling, being the target of racism, but you will have to know what to do once it comes to you. You will have to not be racist toward them because fighting racism with racism will result in hate and further racism, and nothing will get resolved. If you are to think about the formula of no future racism (no future racism = past experiences + change in present thinking + thinking or self-observing) you must apply this formula to the other person as well, so you might better understand the reason why they are acting the way they are. It may be because of their past experience. It may be because they haven't changed their present thinking. It might be because they don't think about or observe themselves.

Change present thinking

I previously mentioned in this section about what causes future racism, using this formula (future racism = past experiences + present thinking + non-thinking or no self-observation), and I explained how a woman that had a bad past experience with a Mexican man, now has this racist thinking towards them all. I explained how she could have spread the reason she hates them to her children. Then her children's children have this thought in their fresh minds.

Fortunately, if one of her children is to cut off this evil curse of thinking racist towards a whole race, this world would be a better place, or at least a start at it. If one of her children is to apply the formula of no future racism (no future racism = past experiences + change in present thinking + thinking or self-observation) then this racism curse would get diluted during his or her children's lifetime. As time goes by their children's children will have no racism toward Mexicans at all. In their vocabulary there will be only the result of no future racism. This could be the case for all ethnic groups.

As J. Krishnamurti said, "It is only when the

mind is free from the old that it meets everything anew, and in that there is joy."

Thinking or self-observing

What would you do if you came across someone that is racist? What would you say? Would you say anything at all? These are questions that you must ask yourself. You never know when, where, or how it could happen.

I believe that if you come across someone that is racist, the best thing to keep in mind is to think and to self-observe yourself. What I mean by this is you must think back to the formula for no future racism (no future racism = past experiences + change in present thinking + thinking or self-observing). When you can train your mind into learning this you will understand that the racist person that is being racist against you thinks in the future racism formula, which is (future racism = past experiences + present thinking + non-thinking or no self-observation). You have to understand they are not perfect, and the best thing to do is walk away from the madness that they are pressuring you with. You must think first, and then you will self-observe your body movement and language that occurs in that particular moment. Because your body only follows your mind. If your mind is clogged with punching that person in the face, then most likely you're not going to have any awareness of your body and just may punch that person or even worse go off in a screaming cussing battle with them. This situation falls into the trust formula. Not the trust formula that's (trust = platonic intimacy + personal interaction) This trust th.t I am going to share with you is specifically for situations that may arise, and you must apply this formula, which is (Trust = willingness to forgive + sympathy for others).

So let me explain this to you more. When you use the formula (Trust = willingness to forgive + sympathy for others) you are using this formula for the reason of not hating a whole racial group, because you came across someone from a different racial group than what you are, and they showed racism towards you. You must use the Trust Formula yourself. You must trust yourself that you can have that willingness to forgive. You must trust yourself that you can have sympathy for others.

If you want to try your best at becoming a person that is not racist, you must use this Trust Formula. However, if you have no trust in the other person and/or yourself and you're not thinking or self-observing then you can begin to transform into being racist toward your own race and or another ethnic group not of your own. I trust that this formula (<u>No Trust</u> = no willingness to forgive + no sympathy for others) can make you racist throughout time if you're not thinking or self-observing yourself constantly.

You never know who could be around watching

you. It could be a child watching you and if they see how, you handled the situation then they will see how to handle that situation if it comes to them. Especially if they are of the same racial group as you are. The child will get a totally different visual perception of his environment, or at least know what to do if a situation arises toward him/her, which is nothing.

If this racist situation happens to you while you are with your child, then you know what to do now. You will have to show them one of Goings Rules of Racism Formula (<u>Trust</u> = willingness to forgive + sympathy for others). And you will have to explain to your daughter or son that you want to be this way because you want to stop the spreading of racism. If they don't understand that, explain it to them.

Cultural Adaptability

Past Experiences

First off, I want to ask you this - What does culture mean to you? What do you believe culture adaptability means? What does culture tolerance mean? After you have taken a moment to think through what these things mean, please continue to read on. If you don't know what these words mean, please continue to read on and I'll explain them.

So, what are cultures? Long story short, it is, "The customs, arts, social institutions, and achievements of a particular nation, people, or other social group."[10]

Cultural adaptability is, according to study.com, "the ability to adapt and understand other cultures within your day-to-day work environment."[11]

This will go hand and hand with what I am going to talk about now. I am going to talk about how having a job can be a little difficult when the people you are working with may be of a different ethnic group than you are. This can be reversed as well. You could have already been at a job and a new person comes in that works with you that is a different racial group than what you are.

For instance, let's use a job where only white people or people that look white have been working for a company for hundreds of years. Then suddenly, a black person applies for a low-level position and gets the job. This past experience of never having a black person working for this company might not be great for this first black person. Maybe most of the people there will not like the fact that there is a black person starting a low-level position because of what they are used to in the past.

Some companies fail to have cultural adaptability with black people. I believe it's because they are used to seeing their own kind only. If they were used to working with black people, then they would not be as racist with them as they are today.

Let's use this article from the guardian.com entitled, "Black former worker awarded $3.2m in Tesla factory racial-harassment suit" (12). Originally awarded $130m, which a judge reduced to $15m, the plaintiff opted for a new trial against the electric vehicle company.[12]

Diaz said in the article that at the Fremont factory they often used racist slurs and scrawled swastikas, racist caricatures, and epithets on walls and work areas.

The employees at the Tesla Fremont factory had a different type of past culture, and it could have been one of hate. This may be so because I believe that hate groups are a form of culture for certain ethnic groups out there. Culture means, "the customs, arts, social institutions, and achievements of a particular nation, people, or other social group," according to Google.com. I am mentioning this because hate groups have customs, arts, social institutions, achievements of a particular nation, people, or other social group. If the person or group has been taught this from generation to generation, then their culture will be with them, which may include hate for other cultures.

Now, there could be a strong possibility that Diaz could think of all white people as being racist.

And this could happen because of the traumatizing experience that happened to him at Tesla's Fremont factory. If he uses this Trust Formula (Trust = willingness to forgive + sympathy for others), I trust that in the back of his mind, when he comes across another friendly, nice white person then he will know that they are not all the same. Diaz will know how to think (Trust = willingness to forgive + sympathy for others), therefore, he could then move into the other Trust Formula. This formula is applied to situations that are with people that are not racist. This could be the change he could work on in his ability to trust. This is the formula (Trust = platonic intimacy + personal interaction)

This is an example for you, because you never know when you might come across a situation where someone of a different racial group acts racist towards you.

Present Thinking

In this section, present thinking, I am going to dive into employment, school, and your interactions with people environments. Within these three topics for this section, I am going to tell you how my theory of formulas could cause future racism for yourself and for the future of others.

When it comes to employment, we all know how to show respect to one another because of the non-discrimination polices that are enforced. Do we truly use culture adaptability to its fullest? What I mean by this is that instead of just saying hi and keep walking how about you seek opportunities to sit down with that person of a different racial background and get to know them and their background? We can sometimes get in that habitual rhythm of superficial interactions. It's all in your present thinking. If you currently think like everyone else, if racism is radiating in the environment, it will keep on being there and will begin to include you. I feel like a lot of people's present thinking is involved with what they see the other person doing. If one person sees another person not asking the other person of a different culture out to an event then it will spread like a mad disease and this will continue for days, months, and maybe even years. Let's use a Muslim person for example. Let's say a job is having an event of some sort and they say before the event that the pizza is getting ordered. All the pizza they are getting are meat lovers' pizzas. No present thinking of the pork that could be on the pizza that that job will be ordering. From what I have learned through some research is that Muslims do not eat pork. How can trust ever happen between the employer and the Muslim person if they may not feel like they are welcome there because of the lack of understanding about their beliefs and culture. This can cause, and continue to reinforce, future racism for both cultures. How can one or the other share trust when the other feels unwanted or misplaced. How can the formula (Trust = platonic intimacy + personal interaction) ever be achieved when you presently think in only your own culture and not mindful of other cultures around you.

School, in this day and age, enrolls many kinds of people, representing many different cultures, different colors of skin, and many different languages. And in most schools that I know of in the United States, they have very high standards for collaboration with other students. If you have the present thinking of only talking to people of your own kind or race, then no one will learn anything about other peoples and cultures, and future racism will continue to thrive. This could happen because of your present thinking that you have in your mind. For instance, you could have sour thoughts of only thinking and collaboration with your own race because it makes you feel safe and warm. All because you had seen them repeatedly in your past. All because you don't want to exercise adapting to change. All this that I mentioned above can cause future racism.

When it comes to interacting with people in your environment of different ethnic groups, it can be a bit frightening. Change in general can be frightening to anyone. When you break through that thin ice of interacting with someone of a different racial group you will eventually get used to it. The only way this thin ice is going to get broken is by listening and showing respect. Trust is another factor in this situation. For example, you must have trust to come up to someone of a different ethnic group that speaks another language and looks different than you do. Trust, using the Trust Formula, will help this continue to happen. The lack of communication with other racial groups is caused by no willingness to forgive and no sympathy for others. (No Trust = no willingness to forgive + no sympathy for others) is the formula that causes no trust. Therefore, the thin ice of getting to know that different racial group will not ever happen. And racism will always linger in the environment.

Let's use this as an example: let's say you open a restaurant and you hire all employees of your own racial group. Everyone there speaking the same language that you are. Everyone there continues with the tradition of only having their kind around working with them. This will no doubt cause future racism. By this happing this will cause a barrier for other racial groups.

Just imagine you are going to apply for a job. You need the money extremely badly. You are on the edge of being homeless. You are about to lose your house. So, you fill out an application, but first you go to see how the environment is. When you see how the environment is you see only one of the same racial groups working for each other. Most likely you will turn around and walk out. Why? I believe you will not feel comfortable working for them because you don't speak their language. Moreover, you will think that you would not fit in. Now what if you go back and tell your friends, family, and any new people that you encountered about your experience. Unfortunately, this will cause racism to spread around. Now what if the person you tell this story to tells someone that he or she is close friends, family, or new people that he or she meets to? Just think of the damage that it could spread around the world. Especially when the person that you have told the story to meets a person of the same racial group. They will have that in the back of their minds when they interact with that racial group. This is where the

Formula of No Trust comes into play. (No Trust = no willingness to forgive + no sympathy for others) This formula is universal, it is connected to each person around the world.

Non-Thinking or No Self-Observation

I see for sure that most hate groups around the world need something to exist. They need a cause to explain their reason why they are how they are. One of their reasons could be when only one racial group gets together and starts something only to benefit their own race. This type of way of doing things would give fuel to the hate groups' fire. I am not going to go into too much more depth about hate groups, but you get what I am talking about. When there is fuel to a hate groups' fire, it cuts off thinking and self-observation. Each day that comes will be filled with racism. This is because they are practicing a piece of the whole formula (Future Racism = past experiences + present thinking + non-thinking or no self-observation). They are using non-thinking and/or no self-observation.

Non-thinking and self-observation are part of the key to what causes racism now and will continue to cause it in the future. Because of someone's non-thinking and non-self-observation, it will be absolutely difficult for a person to see a different racial group as equals. They are more prone to the propaganda of a hate group than ever. They will get lost in their point of view because they don't understand another racial group that's different from their own.

Now, this question is really going to have you thinking, 'Are the people that start their own restaurants, businesses, organizations, who hire only people from their own race, pay only their own, congregate with only their own and don't have anything advertising any different racial group is welcome. Are they any different from a hate group?'

Tolerant

"Willing to accept the beliefs, feelings, habits, or behaviors of another group, culture, etc. as legitimate even when they differ from one's own" This is how the Merriam Webster dictionary defines the word *tolerant*.[13]

In the United States of America there are so many different cultures, beliefs, and racial groups. There was a term used for this and that is 'the melting pot.' "The melting pot is at the heart of the American immigration system. The melting pot comes from the idea that all of the cultural differences in the United States meld together, as if they were metals being melted down to become a stronger alloy."[14]

However, if we as a people living in the United States of America use No Trust Formula and don't tolerant others when we encounter different cultures, racism will continue to thrive. If you use the No Trust Formula (No Trust = no willingness to forgive + no sympathy for others) when meeting with a different culture, then racism will continue to take over the whole world. What do I mean by saying no willingness to forgive? I am saying this because most people get offended by someone that had no idea what they did it. It could have been an accident. For example, someone that is used to saying things with their family or friends, a saying like, 'you are an Indian giver,' may be very offensive to Native Americans. In turn, if the Native American hears this from a different racial group in a joking matter, than they may become racist towards that person's whole racial group. Without having the willingness to forgive misunderstanding the spirit of racism will continue to grow.

Having no sympathy for others, which is the last part of the No Trust Formula, is something that everyone must practice. People can be ignorant in so many ways. For instance, as I mentioned above if that person using that phrase knew they were around a Native American, then they would not have said 'Indian giver' around a Native American. That Native American person must now show that racial group sympathy. Sympathy to the fact that they are ignorant, sympathy to the fact that, they don't know no better, sympathy to the fact that, they will get better only if the there is a believe it will. Once people can pass the No Trust Formula, then they must move up a level to the Trust Formula, which I will explain more later. You know the saying, 'practice makes perfect,' but my saying is this type of practice, moving away from No Trust towards Trust, I truly believe, could help everyone live in harmony.

Racism is like a cancer to this nation. Cancer is terrible, evil, or whatever other negative thing you want to call it. It slowly eats away at people that have given up the fight, destroying them from the inside until they are dead.

Culture Comprehension

If you want culture comprehension in your everyday life you must use it. If you don't use culture comprehension in your life, then you will not put a block on the racism that is currently happening in the United States of America, and around the world. If you try to use culture comprehension and it gets blocked by someone, that is racism. Then the best thing to do is apply the Trust Formula to the situation (Trust = willingness to forgive + sympathy for others)

There may come a time in your life when you apply culture comprehension and the person you are around is racist. Instead of going into the racism trap of No Trust for the whole racial group, therefore, understand that that one person is using the No Trust Formula (No Trust = no willingness to forgive + no sympathy for others), not the entire race or culture that one person represents.

What will happen if everyone refuses to use cultural comprehension positively? Well, I think you know the answer to this question. It will be catastrophic and the spirit of racism will thrive around the world, consuming everyone's mind. I don't want to come across as regimented in any way. I believe for this world to be a better place for the unborn children to come, we must adhere to apply positive culture comprehension. This becomes true when you apply this to any situation that may arise when you encounter a different racial group than your own.

***

Next is the second Goings Rules of Racism experiment for you to do. You may notice that when you are finished your answers may be different than the first experiment. This is most likely due to the knowledge you have gained reading this book. If you continue reading the results section after you take the experiment survey you will understand more about what I am talking about.

Goings Rules of Racism
Experiment 2

Circle # 1   **Circle # 2**   **Circle # 3**

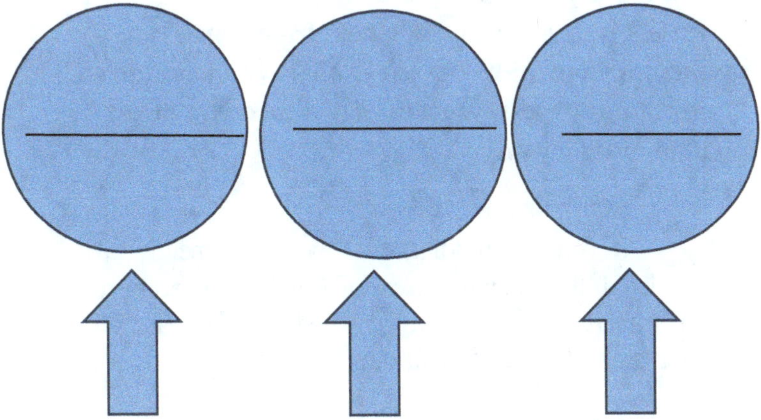

What is your own race?	Your best friend's race or a race you're familiar with?	What is a race you have never collaborated with?

Answer here _______________

My question to you: If you were to do a project or a business venture who would you do it with? Please write your answer to the question right next to the blue arrow pointing at the black line. Please answer circle #1, circle #2, or circle #3. For example, put circle #1 if you would rather do a project or business venture with **your own race**, put circle #2 if you would rather do a project or business venture with **your best friend or a race your familiar with**, put circle #3 if you rather do a project or business venture with **a race you never collaborated with.**

If you are reading this then that means you completed the Goings Rules of Racism Experiment! Congratulations, you are finished. Next you will understand the results of both experiments.

Goings Rules of Racism
Experiment Results

Circle # 1

If you picked your own race, then you're either border line racist, racist and don't know it, or racist and you don't feel comfortable with other races.

You don't use the No Future Racism formula from Goings Rules of Racism. The only formula you're using is the **Future Racism Formula.**

(Future Racism = past experiences + present thinking + non-thinking or no self-observation)

Lastly, you are applying the No Trust Formula to your situation(s).

Trust # 3 (No Trust = no willingness to forgive + sympathy for others)

Circle # 2

If you picked *your best friend's race* or *a race, you're familiar with,* then you're thinking inside the box not outside the box. You will most likely only associate with your own race or racial groups you're familiar with.

You only use **Future Racism** of Goings Rules of Racism Formula, which is (Future Racism = past experiences + present thinking + non-thinking or no self-observation)

You only use this Trust Formula, which is…

Trust # 1 (<u>Trust</u>= platonic intimacy + personal interaction),

Only you use this towards your best friend's race or a race you're familiar with.

Circle # 3

If you picked an *unknown race you've never collaborated with*, you're thinking outside the box. You have a strong sense of adventure, and you want to learn without being biased. You have a strong sense of awareness of the Goings Rules of Racism, which is the **<u>No Future Racism</u>** Formula.

(<u>No Future Racism</u> = past experiences + change present thinking + thinking or self-observation)

Lastly, you are applying the two Trust Formulas to your situation(s).

Trust #1 (<u>Trust</u> = platonic intimacy + personal interaction)

Trust #2 (<u>Trust</u> = willingness to forgive + sympathy for others)

Survey Results

I went out to survey thirty-two people. Eight people in each age group, which are the baby boomers, generation X, generation Y, and generation Z. There were only four age groups, so I found eight people from each age group. Then after I was finished, I added one more person's survey to the bundle. Therefore, there is a total of thirty-three and not thirty-two surveys completed.

The purpose of this experiment in Tacoma and Seattle Washington, is because I wanted to see how people would answer if the questions were asked to them personally and directly from a human being. I wanted to see how people would respond if I made them aware that race was involved in this project. I did this by asking each person four questions:

1)What is your race?
2)What is your best friend's race OR What's a race you're familiar with?
3)What's an unknown race you never collaborated with?
4)If you wanted to do a project or business venture, who would you do it with? I read through the questions I already asked them as their answer choices,

After analyzing and compiling all my results together, age groups 60-78 were high in answering circle 2, *your best friend race or a race you're familiar with.*

For the 44-59 age group, the highest responses were, *it doesn't matter*.

Ages 28-43 had the most answers in the Circle 3 choice, which is, *an unknown race you have never collaborated with.*

It all sounded too good to be true. I felt like they were answering the question that I wanted them to say. I trust that this was because they knew that they were being asked about race and that this experiment is about race.

Lastly, in the 12-27 age range, one thing that I came to the realization is that they seemed more willing to tell you the truth. As I was asking them the survey questions, they answered quickly and with confidence. Many of the answers from the choices after being asked, *if you were to do a project or business venture who would you do it with?* were *your best friend race or a race you're familiar with.*

After I analyzed all of the surveys, I noticed that there were more responses towards the same race than different races. For instance, what I did was count all the participants that picked *for their best friend or a race you're familiar with, choice.* Then I counted all the people that said *the same race as they are* After that I counted all the people that said *a different race than they are.*

My results were that eighteen people said *their same race* or *your best friend or a race you're familiar with*. Fifteen people picked *a different race*. Therefore, there are more people that chose *a best friend or someone they are familiar with*, or *are of the same race* than there are people who chose *a race different than themselves.*

If you look at the results from the Tacoma WA and Seattle WA survey results, you will see that people ages 12-27, the generation Z, answered higher in picking *their best friend's race or a race, you're familiar with* choice when I asked them.

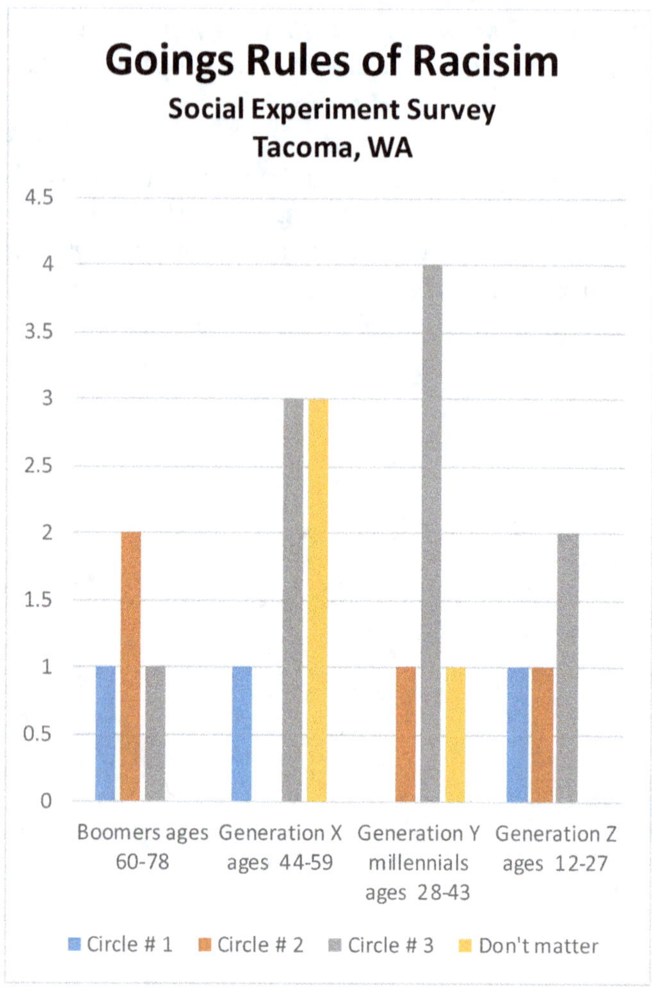
Goings Rules of Racisim
Social Experiment Survey
Tacoma, WA
4.5
4
3.5
3
2.5
2
1.5
1
0.5
0
Boomers ages 60-78
Generation X ages 44-59
Generation Y millennials ages 28-43
Generation Z ages 12-27
Circle # 1
Circle # 2
Circle # 3
Don't matter

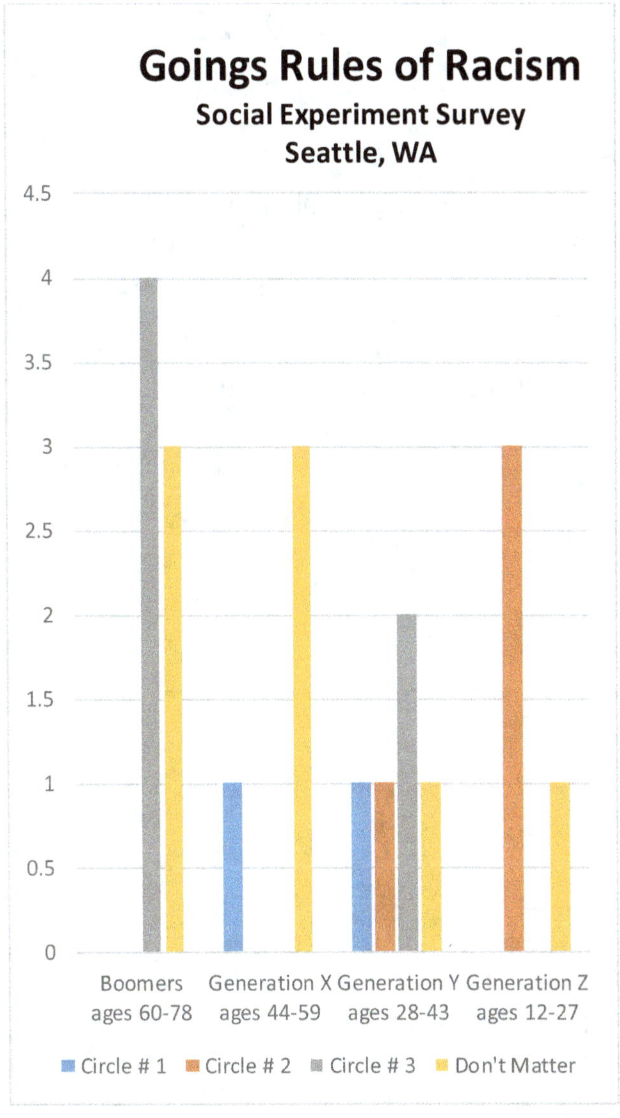

Goings Rules of Racism
Social Experiment Survey
Seattle, WA
4.5
4
3.5
3
2.5
2
1.5
1
0.5
0
Boomers
ages 60-78
Generation X
ages 44-59
Generation Y
ages 28-43
Generation Z
ages 12-27
Circle # 1
Circle # 2
Circle # 3
Don't Matter

Section 2

of Goings Rules of Racism experiment results from survey

The following graph shows all the age groups that answered my questions on Survey Monkey. This is an actual graph from the Survey Money site I used to study the responses and their ages. When I posted the survey on Survey Monkey for individuals to respond to my questions,

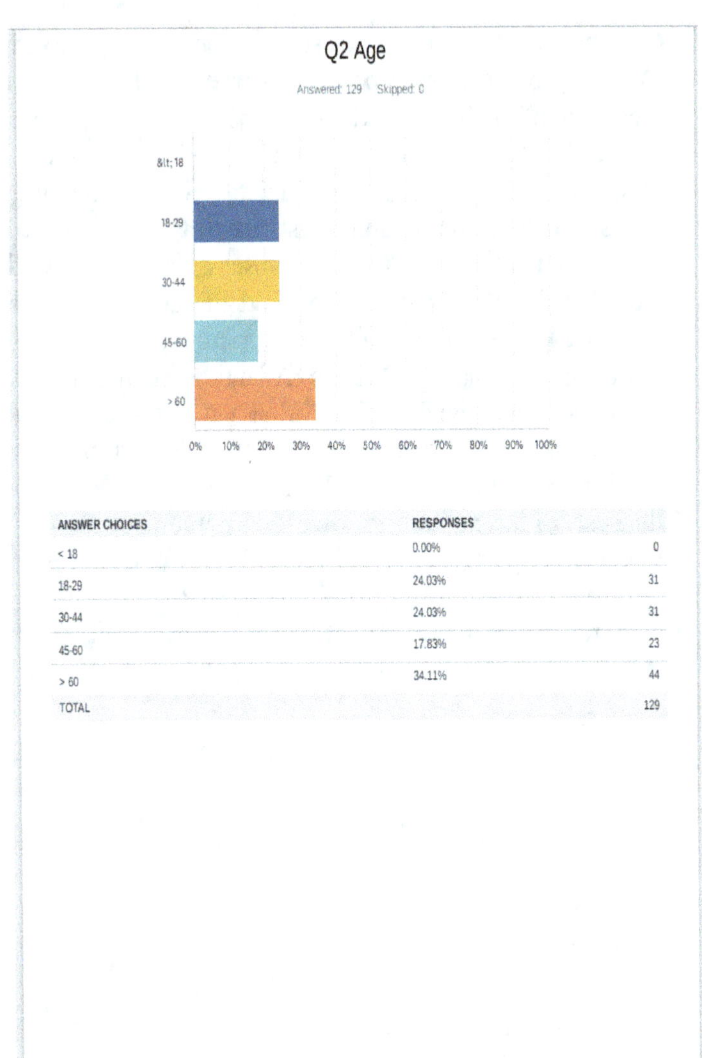

ANSWER CHOICES	RESPONSES	
< 18	0.00%	0
18-29	24.03%	31
30-44	24.03%	31
45-60	17.83%	23
> 60	34.11%	44
TOTAL		129

This next graph represents where the Survey Monkey responses came from. For example, you can see that all 129 respondents came from East North Central, East South Central, Middle Atlantic, Mountain, New England, Pacific, South Atlantic, West North Central, and West South Central. If you draw your attention to the responses section, you will see that there are percentages and the actual number of participants to the right of the percentages.
You will see that the Middle Atlantic was the most in respondents with a 17.97% with twenty-three participants. The rest of the respondents will be respectively following in the order from second highest to the highest to lowest in percentage and number of participants- South Atlantic, Pacific, East North Central, East South Central & West South Central are both tied, West North Central, and Mountain & New England are both tied.

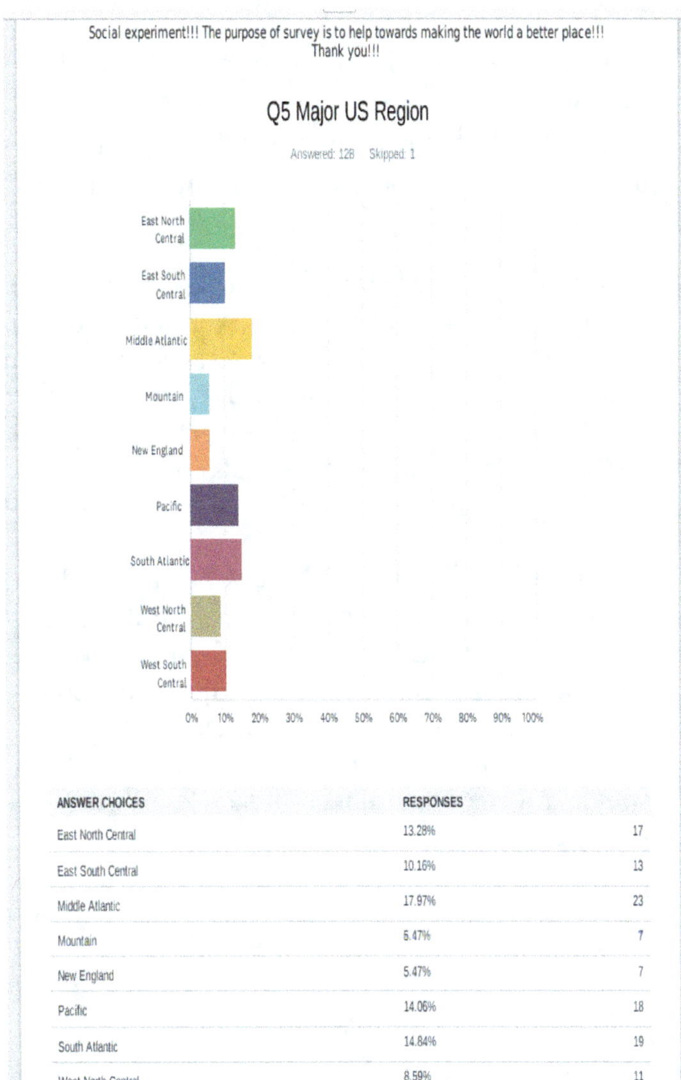

ANSWER CHOICES	RESPONSES	
East North Central	13.28%	17
East South Central	10.16%	13
Middle Atlantic	17.97%	23
Mountain	5.47%	7
New England	5.47%	7
Pacific	14.06%	18
South Atlantic	14.84%	19
West North Central	8.59%	11
West South Central	10.16%	13
TOTAL		128

In the data in the following eight pages, the first four pages are a survey that asks, "What is your race?" The next four pages are responses to the question "What is your best friend's race or another friend's race?".

The way to read these surveys is by matching the numbers on both. For example, the first person answering the first survey is the same person answering the second survey. And so on. Most of the people answered their same race when asked the question, what is your best friends or one of your friend's race? On the second survey.

When I went through the 129 surveys , I wanted to check and see if there were many people that said that their best friends' race was the same as their own race. I was right, by a large majority of people that were asked the question from the survey, *if you want to do a project or business venture who would you do it with?* The majority of the 129 people answered their best friend or friend.

Goings Rules of Racism

Q1 What is your race?

Answered: 129   Skipped: 0

#	RESPONSES	DATE
1	white	2/2/2024 7:10 PM
2	white	2/2/2024 7:10 PM
3	White	2/2/2024 7:10 PM
4	White	2/2/2024 7:10 PM
5	Hispanic	2/2/2024 7:10 PM
6	white	2/2/2024 7:09 PM
7	white	2/2/2024 7:09 PM
8	African American	2/2/2024 7:09 PM
9	Black	2/2/2024 7:09 PM
10	white	2/2/2024 7:09 PM
11	white	2/2/2024 7:09 PM
12	White	2/2/2024 7:09 PM
13	White	2/2/2024 7:09 PM
14	White	2/2/2024 7:09 PM
15	White	2/2/2024 7:09 PM
16	Caucasians	2/2/2024 7:09 PM
17	White	2/2/2024 7:09 PM
18	White	2/2/2024 7:09 PM
19	African American	2/2/2024 7:08 PM
20	Caucasian	2/2/2024 7:07 PM
21	Latino	2/2/2024 7:06 PM
22	White	2/2/2024 6:42 PM
23	Hispanic	2/2/2024 6:41 PM
24	Chinese	2/2/2024 6:12 PM
25	white	2/2/2024 6:04 PM
26	white	2/2/2024 6:02 PM
27	Dhdh	2/2/2024 6:02 PM
28	African American	2/2/2024 5:59 PM
29	Caucasian	2/2/2024 5:41 PM
30	white	2/2/2024 5:41 PM
31	Native	2/2/2024 5:20 PM
32	Latino	2/2/2024 5:17 PM
33	White	2/2/2024 4:57 PM

34	Caucasian	2/2/2024 4:55 PM
35	White	2/2/2024 4:55 PM
36	Human	2/2/2024 4:55 PM
37	Caucasian	2/2/2024 4:55 PM
38	white	2/2/2024 4:54 PM
39	White	2/2/2024 4:54 PM
40	Caucasian	2/2/2024 4:54 PM
41	My father and mother came from German Ancestors	2/2/2024 4:54 PM
42	Black american	2/2/2024 4:54 PM
43	White	2/2/2024 4:53 PM
44	White and Native American	2/2/2024 4:53 PM
45	white	2/2/2024 4:53 PM
46	caucasian	2/2/2024 4:53 PM
47	human	2/2/2024 4:53 PM
48	white	2/2/2024 4:53 PM
49	white	2/2/2024 4:53 PM
50	Asian	2/2/2024 4:52 PM
51	white	2/2/2024 4:52 PM
52	Latino	2/2/2024 4:52 PM
53	white	2/2/2024 4:52 PM
54	White	2/2/2024 4:52 PM
55	White	2/2/2024 4:52 PM
56	Caucasion	2/2/2024 4:52 PM
57	White	2/2/2024 4:52 PM
58	Mixed - primarily caucasian	2/2/2024 4:51 PM
59	White	2/2/2024 4:51 PM
60	white	2/2/2024 4:51 PM
61	White	2/2/2024 4:51 PM
62	African American	2/2/2024 4:51 PM
63	White	2/2/2024 4:51 PM
64	white	2/2/2024 4:50 PM
65	African American	2/2/2024 4:50 PM
66	White	2/2/2024 4:50 PM
67	White	2/2/2024 4:50 PM
68	white	2/2/2024 4:48 PM
69	Caucasian	2/2/2024 4:46 PM
70	White	2/2/2024 4:44 PM
71	White	2/2/2024 4:36 PM

Goings Rules of Racism

72	white	2/2/2024 4:28 PM
73	white	2/2/2024 4:27 PM
74	Cherokee/ Choctaw	2/2/2024 4:27 PM
75	White	2/2/2024 4:27 PM
76	Caucasian	2/2/2024 4:27 PM
77	Caucasian	2/2/2024 4:26 PM
78	Caucasian/Native American	2/2/2024 4:20 PM
79	Black	2/2/2024 4:19 PM
80	White	2/2/2024 4:11 PM
81	White	2/2/2024 4:07 PM
82	Caucasian	2/2/2024 4:03 PM
83	Hispanic	2/2/2024 4:02 PM
84	Black	2/2/2024 3:59 PM
85	African-American	2/2/2024 3:57 PM
86	Caucasian	2/2/2024 3:51 PM
87	America	2/2/2024 3:46 PM
88	Caucasian	2/2/2024 3:42 PM
89	White	2/2/2024 3:39 PM
90	White	2/2/2024 3:29 PM
91	white	2/2/2024 3:26 PM
92	Black	2/2/2024 3:26 PM
93	caucasian	2/2/2024 3:22 PM
94	white	2/2/2024 3:16 PM
95	Hispanic	2/2/2024 3:15 PM
96	White	2/2/2024 3:12 PM
97	White	2/2/2024 3:11 PM
98	White	2/2/2024 3:06 PM
99	white	2/2/2024 3:00 PM
100	white	2/2/2024 2:57 PM
101	White	2/2/2024 2:50 PM
102	Caucasian	2/2/2024 2:42 PM
103	Latino	2/2/2024 2:42 PM
104	Hispanic	2/2/2024 2:41 PM
105	White	2/2/2024 2:32 PM
106	white	2/2/2024 2:29 PM
107	white	2/2/2024 2:29 PM
108	White	2/2/2024 2:29 PM
109	Write	2/2/2024 2:28 PM

Goings Rules of Racism

Social experiment!!! The purpose of survey is to help towards making the world a better place!!!
Thank you!!!

110	White	2/2/2024 2:27 PM
111	white	2/2/2024 2:20 PM
112	white	2/2/2024 2:18 PM
113	White	2/2/2024 2:17 PM
114	White, Hispanic	2/2/2024 2:12 PM
115	democrat	2/2/2024 2:08 PM
116	Caucasian	2/2/2024 1:50 PM
117	White	2/2/2024 1:38 PM
118	White	2/2/2024 1:29 PM
119	white	2/2/2024 1:28 PM
120	Mixed Race	2/2/2024 1:26 PM
121	white	2/2/2024 1:26 PM
122	African American	2/2/2024 1:25 PM
123	Caucasian	2/2/2024 1:25 PM
124	bldg	2/2/2024 1:25 PM
125	White	2/2/2024 1:12 PM
126	white	2/2/2024 1:04 PM
127	white	2/2/2024 1:03 PM
128	hc	2/2/2024 1:03 PM
129	White	2/2/2024 1:03 PM

Q2 What is your best friend's race or one of your friends race?

Answered: 129   Skipped: 0

#	RESPONSES	DATE
1	white	2/2/2024 7:10 PM
2	black	2/2/2024 7:10 PM
3	White	2/2/2024 7:10 PM
4	White	2/2/2024 7:10 PM
5	White	2/2/2024 7:10 PM
6	white	2/2/2024 7:09 PM
7	white	2/2/2024 7:09 PM
8	Caucasian	2/2/2024 7:09 PM
9	Black	2/2/2024 7:09 PM
10	white	2/2/2024 7:09 PM
11	african american	2/2/2024 7:09 PM
12	Ginger	2/2/2024 7:09 PM
13	White	2/2/2024 7:09 PM
14	White	2/2/2024 7:09 PM
15	White	2/2/2024 7:09 PM
16	jar	2/2/2024 7:09 PM
17	White	2/2/2024 7:09 PM
18	White	2/2/2024 7:09 PM
19	African American	2/2/2024 7:08 PM
20	Indian	2/2/2024 7:07 PM
21	Asian	2/2/2024 7:06 PM
22	White	2/2/2024 6:42 PM
23	Hispanic	2/2/2024 6:41 PM
24	White	2/2/2024 6:12 PM
25	African American	2/2/2024 6:04 PM
26	white	2/2/2024 6:02 PM
27	Heheh	2/2/2024 6:02 PM
28	Puerto Rican	2/2/2024 5:59 PM
29	Hispanic and Caucasian	2/2/2024 5:41 PM
30	white	2/2/2024 5:41 PM
31	Norwegian	2/2/2024 5:20 PM
32	María	2/2/2024 5:17 PM
33	Mixed	2/2/2024 4:57 PM

34	Caucasian	2/2/2024 4:55 PM
35	White	2/2/2024 4:55 PM
36	Human	2/2/2024 4:55 PM
37	Caucasian	2/2/2024 4:55 PM
38	white	2/2/2024 4:54 PM
39	White	2/2/2024 4:54 PM
40	Caucasian	2/2/2024 4:54 PM
41	Filipino	2/2/2024 4:54 PM
42	Black american	2/2/2024 4:54 PM
43	White	2/2/2024 4:53 PM
44	White	2/2/2024 4:53 PM
45	mix	2/2/2024 4:53 PM
46	caucasian	2/2/2024 4:53 PM
47	human	2/2/2024 4:53 PM
48	white	2/2/2024 4:53 PM
49	white	2/2/2024 4:53 PM
50	Black	2/2/2024 4:52 PM
51	white	2/2/2024 4:52 PM
52	Latino	2/2/2024 4:52 PM
53	white	2/2/2024 4:52 PM
54	White	2/2/2024 4:52 PM
55	Asian	2/2/2024 4:52 PM
56	Caucasion	2/2/2024 4:52 PM
57	White	2/2/2024 4:52 PM
58	Mixed	2/2/2024 4:51 PM
59	Brown	2/2/2024 4:51 PM
60	white	2/2/2024 4:51 PM
61	White	2/2/2024 4:51 PM
62	African- American	2/2/2024 4:51 PM
63	White	2/2/2024 4:51 PM
64	white	2/2/2024 4:50 PM
65	African American	2/2/2024 4:50 PM
66	White	2/2/2024 4:50 PM
67	White	2/2/2024 4:50 PM
68	white	2/2/2024 4:48 PM
69	Caucasian	2/2/2024 4:46 PM
70	White	2/2/2024 4:44 PM
71	White	2/2/2024 4:36 PM

Goings Rules of Racism

72	white	2/2/2024 4:28 PM
73	white	2/2/2024 4:27 PM
74	White	2/2/2024 4:27 PM
75	White	2/2/2024 4:27 PM
76	African American	2/2/2024 4:27 PM
77	Caucasian	2/2/2024 4:26 PM
78	Caucasian	2/2/2024 4:20 PM
79	Black	2/2/2024 4:19 PM
80	White	2/2/2024 4:11 PM
81	White	2/2/2024 4:07 PM
82	Caucasian	2/2/2024 4:03 PM
83	Hispanic	2/2/2024 4:02 PM
84	Black	2/2/2024 3:59 PM
85	African-American	2/2/2024 3:57 PM
86	Caucasian	2/2/2024 3:51 PM
87	Mexica	2/2/2024 3:46 PM
88	Latino	2/2/2024 3:42 PM
89	White	2/2/2024 3:39 PM
90	White	2/2/2024 3:29 PM
91	philipino	2/2/2024 3:26 PM
92	Black	2/2/2024 3:26 PM
93	same	2/2/2024 3:22 PM
94	white	2/2/2024 3:16 PM
95	Hispanic	2/2/2024 3:15 PM
96	white	2/2/2024 3:12 PM
97	White	2/2/2024 3:11 PM
98	White	2/2/2024 3:06 PM
99	white	2/2/2024 3:00 PM
100	black	2/2/2024 2:57 PM
101	Mixed	2/2/2024 2:50 PM
102	Caucasian	2/2/2024 2:42 PM
103	Latino	2/2/2024 2:42 PM
104	White	2/2/2024 2:41 PM
105	White	2/2/2024 2:32 PM
106	black	2/2/2024 2:29 PM
107	white	2/2/2024 2:29 PM
108	White	2/2/2024 2:29 PM
109	Black	2/2/2024 2:28 PM

Goings Rules of Racism

Social experiment!!! The purpose of survey is to help towards making the world a better place!!!
Thank you!!!

110	White	2/2/2024 2:27 PM
111	white	2/2/2024 2:20 PM
112	white	2/2/2024 2:18 PM
113	Black	2/2/2024 2:17 PM
114	White, Hispanic	2/2/2024 2:12 PM
115	democrat	2/2/2024 2:08 PM
116	Caucasian	2/2/2024 1:50 PM
117	White	2/2/2024 1:38 PM
118	White	2/2/2024 1:29 PM
119	white	2/2/2024 1:28 PM
120	White	2/2/2024 1:26 PM
121	black	2/2/2024 1:26 PM
122	American	2/2/2024 1:25 PM
123	Caucasian	2/2/2024 1:25 PM
124	hadn't	2/2/2024 1:25 PM
125	White	2/2/2024 1:12 PM
126	white	2/2/2024 1:04 PM
127	white	2/2/2024 1:03 PM
128	jhcvv	2/2/2024 1:03 PM
129	White	2/2/2024 1:03 PM

I then analyzed the first question and the second questions, which are, *What is your race?* and, *What is your best friend's race or one of your friends' race?* When I analyzed the second question, *what is your best friend's race or one of your friend's race* from all 129 participants, I noticed something interesting. Sixty-nine participants answered *the same race as themselves* and twenty-two participants picked *a different race then what race they are,* as shown in the chart below.

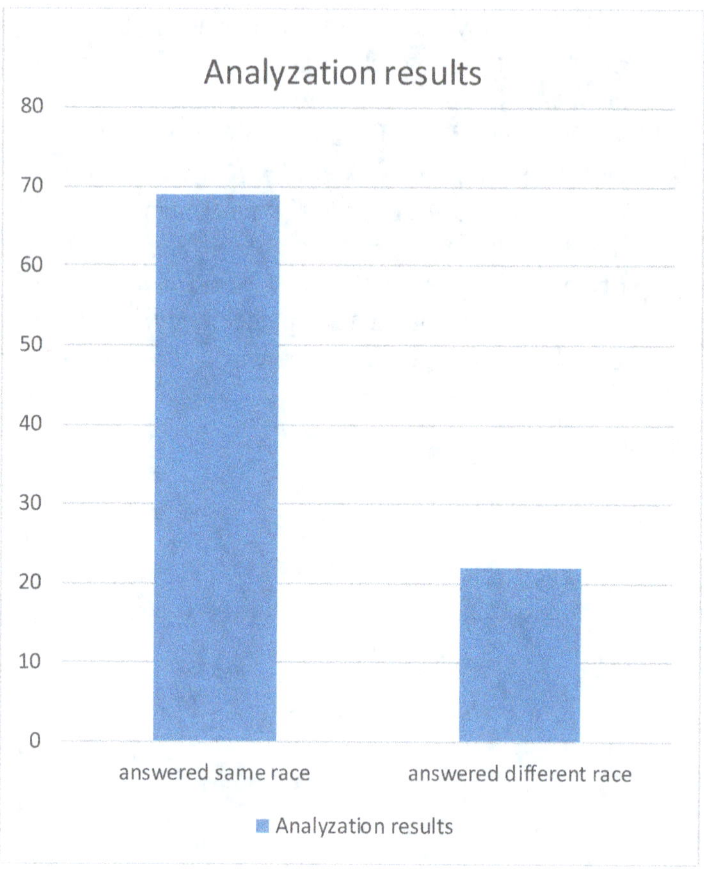

Analyzation results
80
70
60
50
40
30
20
10
0
answered same race
answered different race
Analyzation results

The following graph is the third question I had asked all 129 participants, *if you want to do a project or business venture who would you do it with?*

The participants get to choose between three answer choices. These three choices are: Your own race, your best friend's or a friend's race, or with a person from a racial group you have never interacted with.

As you can see, 19.38% of the responses, twenty-five people, answered *their own race.* 65.89% of the respondents answered, *their best friend or a friend.* For the answer choice, *with a person from a racial group you have never interacted with,* it fell short with only 14.73% of responses, which is nineteen responses out of the 129 participants.

Goings Rules of Racism

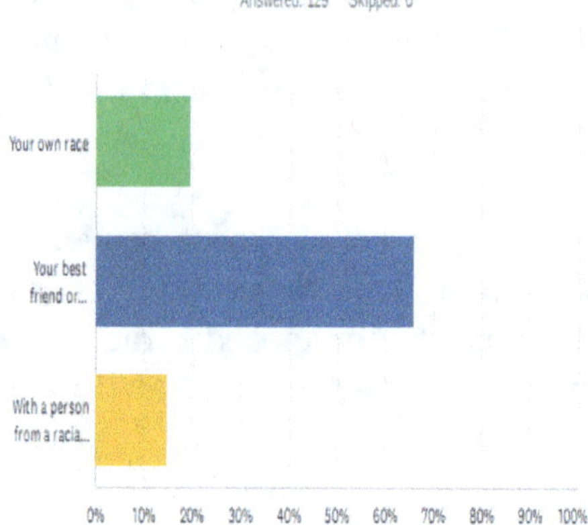

ANSWER CHOICES	RESPONSES	
Your own race	19.38%	25
Your best friend or friend	65.89%	85
With a person from a racial group you have never interacted with.	14.73%	19
TOTAL		129

Below I am going to show you what each question means and what type of person the participants are when they answered the questions. The first bold words are the questions that were on the survey.

Your own race

If, your own race was picked, then they're either boarder line racist, racist and don't know it, or racist and they don't feel comfortable with other races.

They don't use the No Future Racism Formula from Goings Rules of Racism. The only formula they're using is the **Theory of What Causes Future Racism**,

(Future Racism = past experiences + present thinking + non-thinking or no self-observation)

Lastly, they are applying the Trust#3 Formula to their situation(s).

Trust # 3 (No Trust = no willingness to forgive + sympathy for others)

Next, we have…

Best Friend or Friend

If they picked their best friend or friend, then they're thinking inside the box not outside the box. They will most likely only associate with only their own race or racial groups they're familiar with. They will only use **Future Racism Formula.** They fall under the **Theory of What Causes Future Racism**.

(Future Racism = past experiences + present thinking + non-thinking or no self-observation)

They only use this Trust Formula, which is…

Trust # 1 (Trust= platonic intimacy + personal interaction),

They only use this towards their best friend or friend, so it will be their friend's particular race they will only use **Trust #1** towards.

A person from a racial group they have never interacted with.

If they picked this choice, a person from a racial group they have never interacted with, then they are thinking outside the box. They have a strong sense of adventure, and they want to learn without being biased. They have a strong sense of awareness, and they fall under the **Theory of What Causes No Future Racism**.

(No Future Racism = past experiences + change

in present thinking + thinking or self-observation)

Lastly, they are applying the two Trust Formulas to their situation(s).

Trust #1 (<u>Trust</u> = platonic intimacy + personal interaction)

Trust #2 (<u>Trust</u> = willingness to forgive + sympathy for others)

These types of people are very important because they use the No Future Racism, which I believe is the most important formula in the whole world.

<u>No Future Racism & Better World for All & Massive technology</u>= Awareness of visual perceptions + awareness of cultures

This formula is the key to making the world a better place, and when this happens there will be a massive technology advancement beyond our imaginations.

The Boy & The Talking Stone!

There was a black family in a busy mall. The boy that was with his father and mother is thirteen years old. The boy was a curious black boy who was always wondering about why things are the way they are. He would see things and hear things on the news about police killing black men and women. He didn't understand why these things happened.

One day the boy researched who Socrates was and read a little about him. He started to imagine himself as a philosopher. It was late at night, and he went to sleep. While he was asleep, he had a vivid dream.

While dreaming he dreamed that he was wandering off on a desert island. As he was walking all by himself, he stumbled across a beautiful stone. It was massively filled with diamonds, which gave off an amazing sparkle. The stone sparkled so much he had to walk to it. Then the stone gave way to a tone.

"This sound - where is it coming from?" the boy asked himself.

The boy didn't think anything of it. Not until the stone begins to speak in his language.

"Hello, there young man."

"Are you talking?" the boy said to the stone.

"Yes, I can communicate, just like you."

"That's impossible!" the boy said.

"Well, don't you hear me talking to you?" replied the stone.

"Yes, that's impossible, you don't have a mouth like mine." Replied the boy.

"Yes, that is true, but don't you hear me?"

"Yes, I do," replied the boy.

"What is the problem? I can feel that something is wrong. You know your expressions give off energy," said the stone.

"Huh, they do?"

"Yes, why are you wandering all by yourself?" asked the stone.

"I am trying to find an answer to something," said the boy.

"What is the question you're seeking an answer to?" asked the stone.

"Why are people racist?"

"I know exactly the problem."

"What's the problem?"

"Thousands of years passed. Humans stopped connecting to the tone," answered the stone.

"Tone? The tone that I am hearing now?" asked the boy.

"Yes, this is the tone everyone on the planet used to hear. And when they heard it, great things happened. Love was very important, and everyone constantly welcomed transformation into their lives," replied the stone.

"Is it ever going to end?"

"What do you mean? What do you want to end?"

"People hating people because of who they are?"
"Yes, I believe in the future it surely will. When this happens paradise will be upon this planet once again and everyone can tune in to this sound you hear. It will automatically happen."
"This tone sounds like...I don't know. I never heard this sound before," said the boy.

"This sound you hear is what people used to welcome in their hearts, 190,000 years ago. It has been lost to the people now."

hum

"It's a tone we all once were connected to. 528 Hz. It is the purest tone anyone can ever hear. Oh! You are so blessed to hear this sound. It brightens my day at night," said the stone.

"At night?" replied the boy.

"Yes, I rather it be night then day, honestly."

"How do you know all of this?" asked the boy.

"Young man, do you know how old I am?"

"No, how old are you?"

"I am 4.2 billion years old. Every year that passed by me I have counted," replied the stone.

"Hum, that's impossible!"

"What is impossible? Is there a such thing as that word? What I have seen is that everything is possible," replied the stone.

"You said everything is possible."

"Yes, I lived in the time of Atlantica!" said the stone.

"Atlantica? What is that? I heard of it before. I think," said the boy.

"Atlantica or Atlantis... Atlantis is probably what you've heard. It was a great time for humans." The boy sat down next to the large triangular stone. His eyes grew larger, and his eyes were fixed on the massive stone. He was so comfortable because of the sound of the tone. He took a deep inhale and exhaled with great concentration on what the stone was saying.

"Humans lived very long lives. They lived to

almost reach 1,000 years old," said the stone.

"1,000 years old?" the boy asked.

"Yes!"

"How did people look back then?" asked the curious boy.

"Back then people all had a dark complexion," replied the stone.

"The tone was heard in the minds and souls of every living being on this planet. It gave people great thinking abilities. Miracles happened, love was high, and people were obsessed with transforming into something better than what they were the day before. The people had no stress, and the technology was great. It was beyond your imagination. Everything that you could think of became possible."

"I wish I lived in Atlantis!" replied the boy.

"So, to answer your question. You asked me will racism ever end, yes it surely will. Once people find the tone, once people open their minds, once people work together as one. That's when paradise will be on earth again," said the stone.

<u>Theories</u>

1) Theory of what causes **<u>future racism</u>**!

2) Theory of what causes **<u>no future racism</u>**!

<u>Goings Rules of Racism</u>
<u>Formulas</u>

1) <u>No Future Racism</u>= past experiences +
    change in present thinking + thinking or self-
    observation

2) <u>Future Racism</u>= past experiences + present
    thinking + non-thinking or no self-
    observation

3) <u>No Future Racism & Better World for all &
    Massive Technology</u>= Awareness of visual
    perceptions + awareness of cultures

<u>Trust Formulas</u>

Trust Formula 1: <u>Trust</u> = platonic intimacy + personal interaction

Applied to situations that are with people that are not racist. This could be a chance to work on your ability to trust.

Trust Formula 2: <u>Trust</u> = willingness to forgive + sympathy for others

Applied to situations that may arise if you encounter a racist person. How to react to them after you felt discriminated against.

Trust Formula 3: <u>No trust</u> = no willingness to forgive + no sympathy for others

This is the cause that begins to transform people into being racist towards different racial groups, sometimes even your own race.

ABOUT THE AUTHOR

Preston A. Goings is an author, film director, producer, writer and inventor. Preston A. Goings was born in Renton, Washington, and raised in Peoria, Illinois. When Preston was young, he would always draw and write inside his journal.

Preston received his MFA in Filmmaking and Producing from Seattle Film Institute. He loves to see the world as a better place and strives to help contribute to the world. He loves to do this from his movies and inventions. One invention he has published U.S. Patent Application No. US 2024/0212839 A1 for Psychotherapy device.

Preston has multiple projects he is working on. One of the projects he is currently working on is called, "Car Show Rivalry" He has self-published multiple books on Amazon. One of his books is called, "Car Show Rivalry".

For Preston Goings's amazon author page scan QR code.

Endnotes

1. "Confronting Indirect Racism - Racism - Issues Online." *Www.issuesonline.co.uk*, accessed February 24, 2024, www.issuesonline.co.uk/articles/confronting-indirect-racism-5488.

2. Tanja McIlroy, "12 Visual Perception Activities for Kids - Empowered Parents," Empowered Parents, November 13, 2023, accessed February 24, 2024, https://empoweredparents.co/12-ideas-to-develop-your-childs-visual-perception/#:~:text=An%20example%20of%20visual%20perception%20is%20when%20a%20child%20reads,memorize%20some%20of%20these%20forms

3. Sasha Blakeley, *"Visual Perception: Definition, Theories, & Importance,"* Study.com, last modified November 21, 2023, accessed February 24, 2024, https://study.com/learn/lesson/visual-perception-overview-examples.html

4. Kelsey Schultz, *"Self-Image: Definition, Issues, & Tips,"* The Berkeley Well-Being Institute, accessed February 24, 2024, https://www.berkeleywellbeing.com/self-image.html

5. Michelle Toh, Candice Zhu, and Gawon Bae, *"'The Little Mermaid' Tanks in China and South Korea amid Racist Backlash from Some Viewers,"* CNN Business, June 6, 2023,accessed October 1, 2023, www.cnn.com/2023/06/06/media/little-mermaid-box-office-china-korea-intl-hnk/index.html.

6. Jason Dorsey, *"Generation FAQ's,"* Jasondorsey.com, accessed February 24, 2024, https://jasondorsey.com/about-generations/generations-birth-years/

7. Yoonji Han, *"I'd always fantasized about living in Japan. But after nearly 3 years of living here as a black woman, I'm ready to move back to the US,"* MSN.com, accessed February 24, 2024, https://www.msn.com/en-us/news/other/i-d-always-fantasized-about-living-in-japan-but-after-nearly-3-years-of-living-here-as-a-black-woman-i-m-ready-to-move-back-to-the-us/ar-AA1gdpaj?ocid=msedgntp&cvid=453903d2cfbc453981e15e725e7a4c9d&ei=52

8."Definition of 'subconscious," *Collins,* accessed February 24, 2024, https://www.collinsdictionary.com/us/dictionary/english/subconscious

9.Victoria Sebastian, *"Secrets of the Subconcious,"* Reporter.rit.edu, published February 2, 2021, Accessed February 24, 2024, https://reporter.rit.edu/features/secrets-subconscious

10. "Culture," *Oxford Dictionary,* accessed February 24, 2024, https://www.google.com/search?q=culture+definition&sca_esv=72ff9969706166be&sxsrf=ACQVn0_PGrWtnvz5t-SRmPwfF177N72vJA%3A1708811341886&source=hp&ei=TWTaZdn4M9DWkPIPrOW2qAU&iflsig=ANes7DEAAAAAZdpyXXeWQWXm3uW0nnfcvSsF38ayD8

hv&oq=culture+&gs_lp=Egdnd3Mtd2l6IghjdWx0dXJlll
CoCCAIyCxAAGIAEGIoFGJECMg4QLhiABBixAxjH
ARjRAzIIEAAYgAQYsQMyCBAAGIAEGLEDMgsQ
LhiABBixAxiDATILEAAYgAQYsQMYgwEyDhAuGI
AEGLEDGMcBGNEDMgsQLhiABBjHARivATIFEAA
YgAQyCxAuGIAEGMcBGK8BSPJZUJQrWONHcAF4
AJABAJgBeKABuAaqAQM1LjO4AQHIAQD4AQGY
AgmgAuoGqAIKwgIHECMY6gIYJ8ICChAjGIAEGIo
FGCfCAhEQLhiABBixAxiDARjHARjRA8ICDhAuGI
AEGIoFGLEDGIMBwgIKEAAYgAQYigUYQ8ICDR
AAGIAEGIoFGEMYsQPCAhEQLhiABBixAxiDARjH
ARivAcICCBAuGIAEGLEDwgIWEC4YgAQYigUYs
QMYgwEYxwEY0QMYCsICDhAAGIAEGIoFGJECG
LEDwgIKEAAYgAQYFBiHAsICERAAGIAEGIoFGJ
ECGLEDGMkDwgILEAAYgAQYigUYkgPCAg4QLhj
HARixAxjRAxiABJgDCJIHAzQuNQ&sclient=gws-wiz

11. Joseph Madison, *"Cultural Adaptability: Definition & Development,"* Study.com, accessed February 24, 2024, https://study.com/academy/lesson/cultural-adaptability-definition-development.html

12. Kari Paul, *"Black former worked awarded $3.2m in Tesla factory racial-harassment suit,"* TheGuardian.com, published Paril 3, 2023, accessed February 24, 2024, https://www.theguardian.com/us-news/2023/apr/03/tesla-racial-harassment-lawsuit-award-california-factory

13. "Tolerant," *Merriam-Webster Dictionary,* . Merriam-Webster.com, accessed February 24, 2024, www.merriam-webster.com/dictionary/tolerant.

14. "Why is America Called the Melting Pot?," Golden Beacon USA.com, published October 30th, 2020, accessed February 24, 2024, https://goldenbeaconusa.com/why-is-america-called-the-melting-pot/#:~:text=The%20melting%20pot%20is%20at,to%20become%20a%20stronger%20alloy.

Goings Rules of Racism

Group Study

There will be three parts to this group study. After you have completed this group study, I hope that you will have new friends and will be thinking outside of the box, with a great sense of awareness. Please pay close attention to the group study rules. Thank you, and please have fun!

Group Study Rules!

1) Try to include people who aren't that familiar with each other's beliefs, which will aid in more honest, open dialogue.

2) Try to have more than one race represented in your study group.

3) Avoid getting angry, arguing, or being disrespectful of each other. We all come from different backgrounds and upbringings!

4) Try to have at least three people participate in your study. With at least two races/cultures represented.

5) Everyone participates, including the person presenting the group study.

6) Work on thinking outside the box when conversating with each other.

Exercises:

1. Read a section or two and discuss your feelings about the material presented. What is something NEW you've learned in the chapter/s?

2. As you encounter each formula, discuss it. How does each part of the formula lead one to the formula's result? Do you agree or disagree?

3. Go through the Goings Rules of Racism experiment. There will be three parts to this group study for a true completion. After you all have completed this group study, I hope that you will have new friends and will be thinking outside of the box, with a great sense of awareness. Please pay close attention to the group study rules. Thank you, please have fun!

Additional inspirational & self-help books

Scan QR code or visit Amazon.com

A Guidebook for
Surviving and Breaking
Free from Being Homeless
How to survive
sleeping in a tent!
How to get a job!
Ideas for getting out
of homelessness!
How to get help if you're
addicted to drugs!
Learn about the four
types of homelessness!
How to survive
sleeping in your car!
Preston A Goings

9 798888 298446